MY SERMON NOTES

52 WEEKS OF CREATIVE NOTE-TAKING FOR BOYS AGES 7+

MY SERMON NOTES FOR BOYS

52 Weeks of Creative Note – Taking for Boys Ages 7+

ISBN: 9798713192853

This Sermon Journal Belongs to:

_____

_____

_____

Help your kids focus on Sunday Services in the most creative and engaging way!

This Sermon Notes Journal provides **104 uniquely designed pages** with fun questions to answer and reflect on. This will help you keep your kid's mind active while focusing on Sunday Services.

This Sermon Notes Journal also acts as a keepsake to record your kid's notes and thoughts that they can look back on for years to come.

Key Features of our Book

Holds 52 Sermons
(2 Beautiful Pages for Each Sermon)
NON-REPETITIVE DESIGNS

Page 1  Page 2

Our design provides different themes and activities that your kids might enjoy doing whether it is sports-related, self-care, love for animals, love for nature, and any other interesting activities.

At the end of the Sermon, your kids will learn to listen, reflect, learn and apply the word of God in their lives.

We are happy to help! We appreciate a review from you! Be blessed and be a blessing!

TO PARENTS & GUARDIAN

"Train up a child in the way he should go, And when he is old he will not depart from it."

Proverbs 22:6

TO CHILDREN

"Children, obey your parents in the Lord, for this is right. "Honor your father and mother," which is the first commandment with a promise: "that it may be well with you, and you may live long on the earth."

Ephesians 6:1-4

My Sermon Notes

Date:

Speaker:

Today's Scripture?

Book:

Chapter:

Verse(s):

How do you watch the sermon?

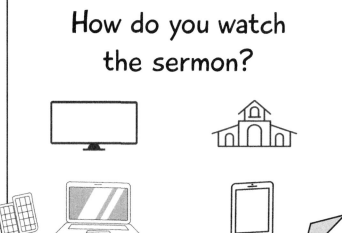

3 BIG THINGS I LEARNED TODAY:

Who you watched the sermon with?

Words I don't know:

DRAW A PICTURE OF SOMETHING YOU HEARD IN THE SERMON

SERMON NOTES

Date: _____   Speaker: _____

Bible Scripture: _____

3 WORDS I HEARD MORE THAN ONCE:

1.

2.

3.

WHAT ARE YOU LEARNING ABOUT GOD FROM THIS SERMON?

I can use this in my life by..

WORDS I HEARD BUT DON'T KNOW:

MY FAVORITE
WORSHIP SONG TODAY:

FUTURE
PILOT!

A GOOD VERSE
TO REMEMBER:

SOMETHING I LEARNED ABOUT MYSELF

My Sermon Notes

BIBLE PASSAGE

Book:

Chapter:

Verse(s):

Speaker:

Location:

WHAT I LEARNED

Who are the main characters in the passage?

What does God want me to learn?

GO TEAM

How should I change because of this sermon?

My favorite worship song today:

Today I want to pray for:

GO TEAM

DRAW A PICTURE OR WRITE SOMETHING YOU HEARD IN THE SERMON

My Sermon Notes

	YES!	NO!
Did you read your Bible this week?	☐	☐
Did you still remember last week's sermon?	☐	☐
Can you say a verse you have learned recently?	☐	☐

BIBLE PASSAGE: **DATE:**

CATCH THE WORD: Check the box each time you hear the word.

☐ God   ☐ Pray   ☐ Obey
☐ Love   ☐ Hope   ☐ Faith
☐ Jesus   ☐ Savior   ☐ Repent
☐ Believe   ☐ Truth   ☐ Joy

TODAY'S SERMON IS ABOUT..

APPLICATION

I should..

I should not..

DRAW A PICTURE OF SOMETHING YOU HEARD IN THE SERMON

My Sermon Notes

Date:

Speaker:

Today's Scripture?

Book:

Chapter:

Verse(s):

How do you watch the sermon?

3 BIG THINGS I LEARNED TODAY:

Who you watched the sermon with?

Words I don't know:

DRAW A PICTURE OF SOMETHING YOU HEARD IN THE SERMON

SERMON NOTES

Date: _____   Speaker: _____

Bible Scripture: _____

3 WORDS I HEARD MORE THAN ONCE:

1.

2.

3.

WHAT ARE YOU LEARNING ABOUT GOD FROM THIS SERMON?

I can use this in my life by..

WORDS I HEARD BUT DON'T KNOW:

MY FAVORITE WORSHIP SONG TODAY:

Happy Robots!

A GOOD VERSE TO REMEMBER:

SOMETHING I LEARNED ABOUT MYSELF

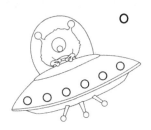

My Sermon Notes

BIBLE PASSAGE

Book:

Chapter:

Verse(s):

Speaker:

Location:

WHAT I LEARNED

Who are the main characters in the passage?

What does God want me to learn?

How should I change because of this sermon?

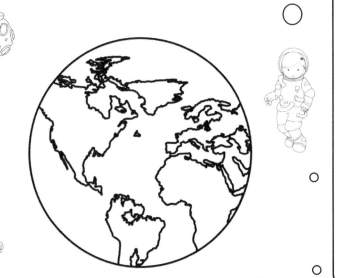

My favorite worship song today:

Today I want to pray for:

DRAW A PICTURE OR WRITE SOMETHING YOU HEARD IN THE SERMON

My Sermon Notes

	YES!	NO!
Did you read your Bible this week?	☐	☐
Did you still remember last week's sermon?	☐	☐
Can you say a verse you have learned recently?	☐	☐

BIBLE PASSAGE: DATE:

CATCH THE WORD: Check the box each time you hear the word.

☐ God   ☐ Pray   ☐ Obey
☐ Love   ☐ Hope   ☐ Faith
☐ Jesus   ☐ Savior   ☐ Repent
☐ Believe   ☐ Truth   ☐ Joy

TODAY'S SERMON IS ABOUT..

APPLICATION

I should..

I should not..

DRAW A PICTURE OF SOMETHING YOU HEARD IN
THE SERMON

My Sermon Notes

Date:

Speaker:

Today's Scripture?

Book:

Chapter:

Verse(s):

How do you watch the sermon?

3 BIG THINGS I LEARNED TODAY:

Who you watched the sermon with?

Words I don't know:

DRAW A PICTURE OF SOMETHING YOU HEARD IN THE SERMON

Bonjour
PARIS

BOULANGERIE
DE PARIS

SERMON NOTES

Date: _____   Speaker: _____

Bible Scripture: _____

3 WORDS I HEARD MORE THAN ONCE:

1.

2.

3.

WHAT ARE YOU LEARNING ABOUT GOD FROM THIS SERMON?

I can use this in my life by..

WORDS I HEARD BUT DON'T KNOW:

MY FAVORITE WORSHIP SONG TODAY:

A GOOD VERSE TO REMEMBER:

SOMETHING I LEARNED ABOUT MYSELF

My Sermon Notes

BIBLE PASSAGE

Book:

Chapter:

Verse(s):

Speaker:

Location:

WHAT I LEARNED

Who are the main characters in the passage?

What does God want me to learn?

How should I change because of this sermon?

My favorite worship song today:

Today I want to pray for:

DRAW A PICTURE OR WRITE SOMETHING YOU HEARD IN THE SERMON

My Sermon Notes

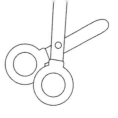

	YES!	NO!
Did you read your Bible this week?	☐	☐
Did you still remember last week's sermon?	☐	☐
Can you say a verse you have learned recently?	☐	☐

BIBLE PASSAGE: DATE:

CATCH THE WORD: Check the box each time you hear the word.

☐ God   ☐ Pray   ☐ Obey
☐ Love   ☐ Hope   ☐ Faith
☐ Jesus   ☐ Savior   ☐ Repent
☐ Believe   ☐ Truth   ☐ Joy

TODAY'S SERMON IS ABOUT..

APPLICATION

I should..

I should not..

DRAW A PICTURE OF SOMETHING YOU HEARD IN THE SERMON

My Sermon Notes

Date:

Speaker:

Today's Scripture?

Book:

Chapter:

Verse(s):

How do you watch the sermon?

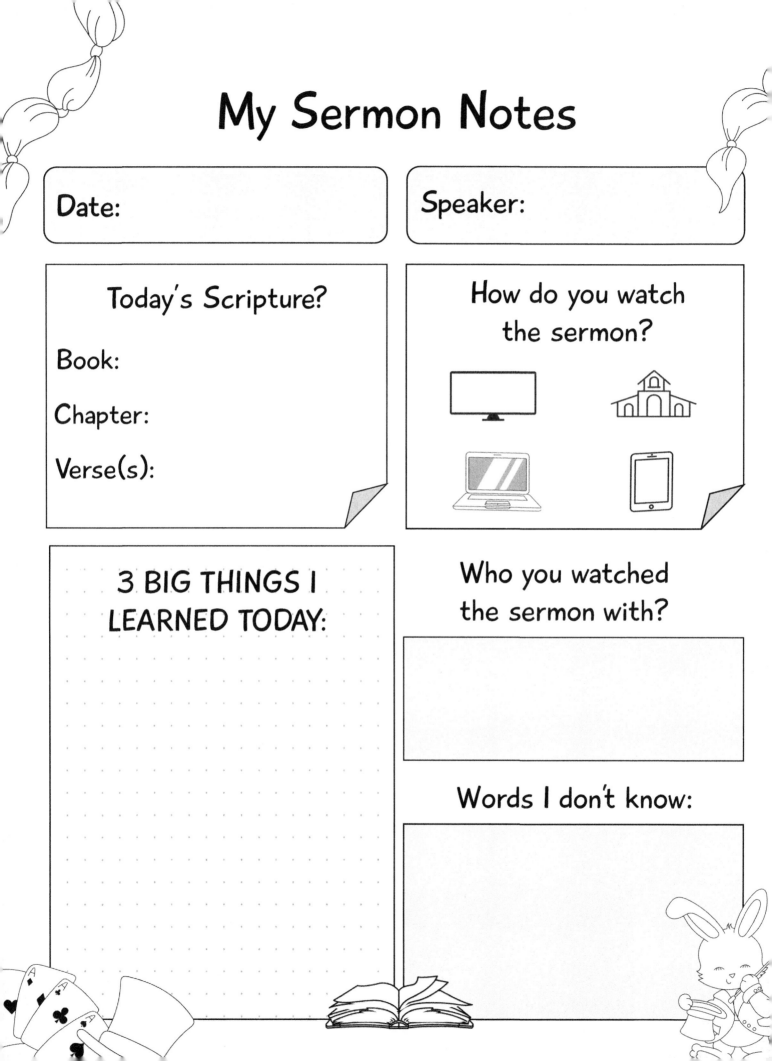

3 BIG THINGS I LEARNED TODAY:

Who you watched the sermon with?

Words I don't know:

DRAW A PICTURE OF SOMETHING YOU HEARD IN THE SERMON

SERMON NOTES

Date: _____   Speaker: _____

Bible Scripture: _____

3 WORDS I HEARD MORE THAN ONCE:

1.

2.

3.

WHAT ARE YOU LEARNING ABOUT GOD FROM THIS SERMON?

I can use this in my life by..

WORDS I HEARD BUT DON'T KNOW:

MY FAVORITE WORSHIP SONG TODAY:

A GOOD VERSE TO REMEMBER:

SOMETHING I LEARNED ABOUT MYSELF

My Sermon Notes

BIBLE PASSAGE

Book:

Chapter:

Verse(s):

Speaker:

Location:

WHAT I LEARNED

Who are the main characters in the passage?

What does God want me to learn?

How should I change because of this sermon?

CAMP LIFE!

My favorite worship song today:

Today I want to pray for:

DRAW A PICTURE OR WRITE SOMETHING YOU HEARD IN THE SERMON

My Sermon Notes

YES! NO!

Did you read your Bible this week? ☐ ☐

Did you still remember last week's sermon? ☐ ☐

Can you say a verse you have learned recently? ☐ ☐

BIBLE PASSAGE: DATE:

CATCH THE WORD: Check the box each time you hear the word.

☐ God   ☐ Pray   ☐ Obey
☐ Love   ☐ Hope   ☐ Faith
☐ Jesus   ☐ Savior   ☐ Repent
☐ Believe   ☐ Truth   ☐ Joy

TODAY'S SERMON IS ABOUT..

APPLICATION

I should..

I should not..

DRAW A PICTURE OF SOMETHING YOU HEARD IN THE SERMON

My Sermon Notes

Date:

Speaker:

Today's Scripture?

Book:

Chapter:

Verse(s):

How do you watch the sermon?

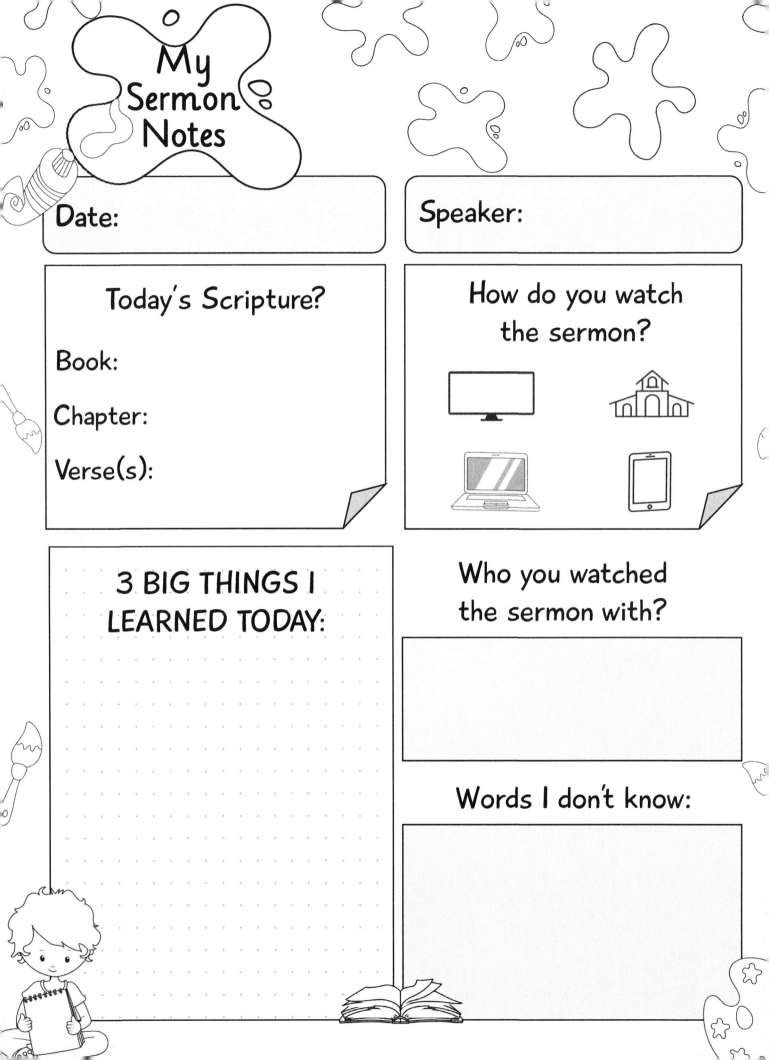

3 BIG THINGS I LEARNED TODAY:

Who you watched the sermon with?

Words I don't know:

DRAW A PICTURE OF SOMETHING YOU HEARD IN THE SERMON

SERMON NOTES

Date: _____   Speaker: _____

Bible Scripture: _____

3 WORDS I HEARD MORE THAN ONCE:

1.

2.

3.

WHAT ARE YOU LEARNING ABOUT GOD FROM THIS SERMON?

I can use this in my life by..

WORDS I HEARD BUT DON'T KNOW:

APPLE PICKING!

MY FAVORITE
WORSHIP SONG TODAY:

A GOOD VERSE
TO REMEMBER:

SOMETHING I LEARNED ABOUT MYSELF

My Sermon Notes

BIBLE PASSAGE

Book:

Chapter:

Verse(s):

Speaker:

Location:

WHAT I LEARNED

Who are the main characters in the passage?

What does God want me to learn?

How should I change because of this sermon?

POPCORN

CIRCUS LIFE!

My favorite worship song today:

Today I want to pray for:

DRAW A PICTURE OR WRITE SOMETHING YOU HEARD IN THE SERMON

My Sermon Notes

Did you read your Bible this week?

YES! ☐ NO! ☐

Did you still remember last week's sermon?

YES! ☐ NO! ☐

Can you say a verse you have learned recently?

YES! ☐ NO! ☐

BIBLE PASSAGE: **DATE:**

CATCH THE WORD: Check the box each time you hear the word.

- ☐ God
- ☐ Love
- ☐ Jesus
- ☐ Believe

- ☐ Pray
- ☐ Hope
- ☐ Savior
- ☐ Truth

- ☐ Obey
- ☐ Faith
- ☐ Repent
- ☐ Joy

TODAY'S SERMON IS ABOUT..

APPLICATION

I should..

I should not..

DRAW A PICTURE OF SOMETHING YOU HEARD IN THE SERMON

My Sermon Notes

Date:

Speaker:

Today's Scripture?

Book:

Chapter:

Verse(s):

How do you watch the sermon?

3 BIG THINGS I LEARNED TODAY:

Who you watched the sermon with?

Words I don't know:

DRAW A PICTURE OF SOMETHING YOU HEARD IN THE SERMON

SERMON NOTES

Date: _____   Speaker: _____

Bible Scripture: _____

3 WORDS I HEARD MORE THAN ONCE:

1.

2.

3.

WHAT ARE YOU LEARNING ABOUT GOD FROM THIS SERMON?

I can use this in my life by..

WORDS I HEARD BUT DON'T KNOW:

MY FAVORITE WORSHIP SONG TODAY:

A GOOD VERSE TO REMEMBER:

SOMETHING I LEARNED ABOUT MYSELF

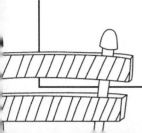
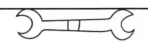

My Sermon Notes

BIBLE PASSAGE

Book:

Chapter:

Verse(s):

Speaker:

Location:

WHAT I LEARNED

Who are the main characters in the passage?

What does God want me to learn?

How should I change because of this sermon?

KARATE

TRAIN   PROGRESS

My favorite worship song today:

Today I want to pray for:

TRAIN

DRAW A PICTURE OR WRITE SOMETHING YOU HEARD IN THE SERMON

PROGRESS

My Sermon Notes

	YES!	NO!
Did you read your Bible this week?	☐	☐
Did you still remember last week's sermon?	☐	☐
Can you say a verse you have learned recently?	☐	☐

BIBLE PASSAGE: **DATE:**

CATCH THE WORD: Check the box each time you hear the word.

☐ God   ☐ Pray   ☐ Obey
☐ Love   ☐ Hope   ☐ Faith
☐ Jesus   ☐ Savior   ☐ Repent
☐ Believe   ☐ Truth   ☐ Joy

TODAY'S SERMON IS ABOUT..

APPLICATION

I should..

I should not..

DRAW A PICTURE OF SOMETHING YOU HEARD IN THE SERMON

My Sermon Notes

Date:

Speaker:

Today's Scripture?

Book:

Chapter:

Verse(s):

How do you watch the sermon?

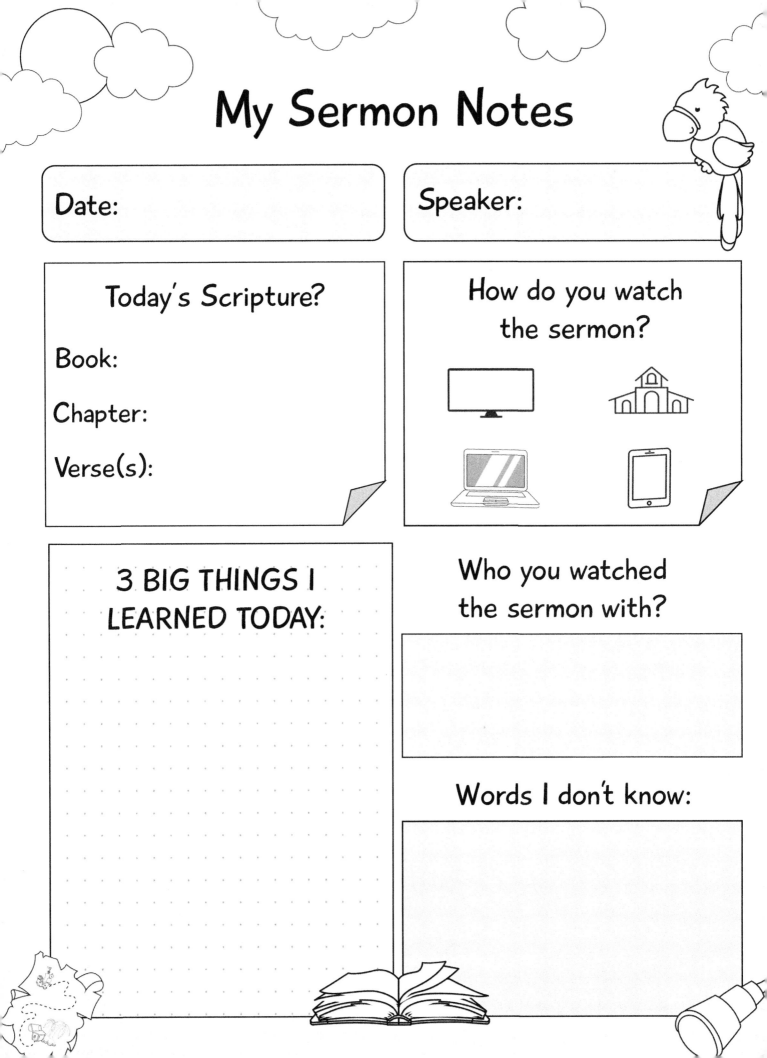

3 BIG THINGS I LEARNED TODAY:

Who you watched the sermon with?

Words I don't know:

DRAW A PICTURE OF SOMETHING YOU HEARD IN THE SERMON

SERMON NOTES

Date: _____ Speaker: _____

Bible Scripture: _____

3 WORDS I HEARD MORE THAN ONCE:

1.

2.

3.

WHAT ARE YOU LEARNING ABOUT GOD FROM THIS SERMON?

I can use this in my life by..

WORDS I HEARD BUT DON'T KNOW:

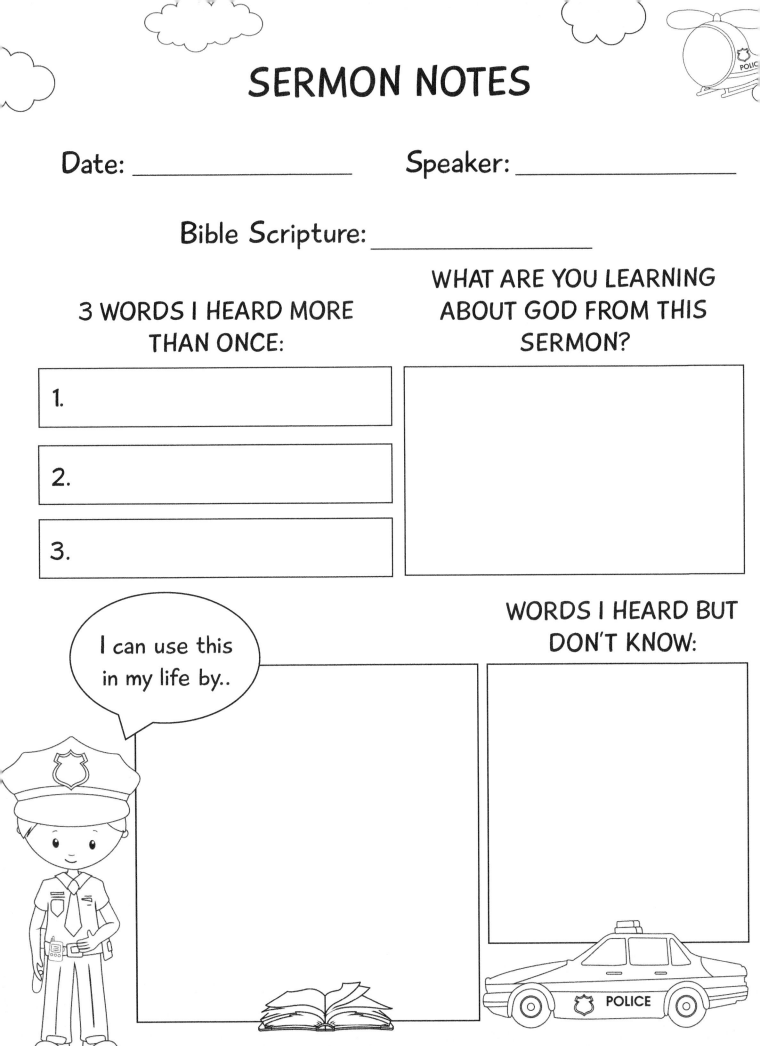

MY FAVORITE WORSHIP SONG TODAY:

A GOOD VERSE TO REMEMBER:

SOMETHING I LEARNED ABOUT MYSELF

My Sermon Notes

BIBLE PASSAGE

Book:

Chapter:

Verse(s):

Speaker:

Location:

WHAT I LEARNED

Who are the main characters in the passage?

What does God want me to learn?

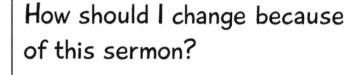

How should I change because of this sermon?

My favorite worship song today:

Today I want to pray for:

DRAW A PICTURE OR WRITE
SOMETHING YOU HEARD IN THE
SERMON

My Sermon Notes

	YES!	NO!
Did you read your Bible this week?	☐	☐
Did you still remember last week's sermon?	☐	☐
Can you say a verse you have learned recently?	☐	☐

BIBLE PASSAGE: DATE:

CATCH THE WORD: Check the box each time you hear the word.

❏ God	❏ Pray	❏ Obey
❏ Love	❏ Hope	❏ Faith
❏ Jesus	❏ Savior	❏ Repent
❏ Believe	❏ Truth	❏ Joy

TODAY'S SERMON IS ABOUT..

APPLICATION

I should..

I should not..

DRAW A PICTURE OF SOMETHING YOU HEARD IN THE SERMON

My Sermon Notes

Date:

Speaker:

Today's Scripture?

Book:

Chapter:

Verse(s):

How do you watch the sermon?

3 BIG THINGS I LEARNED TODAY:

Who you watched the sermon with?

Words I don't know:

DRAW A PICTURE OF SOMETHING YOU HEARD IN THE SERMON

SERMON NOTES

Date: _____   Speaker: _____

Bible Scripture: _____

3 WORDS I HEARD MORE THAN ONCE:

1.

2.

3.

WHAT ARE YOU LEARNING ABOUT GOD FROM THIS SERMON?

I can use this in my life by..

WORDS I HEARD BUT DON'T KNOW:

PRAISE & WORSHIP

MY FAVORITE WORSHIP SONG TODAY:

PRAISE & WORSHIP

A GOOD VERSE TO REMEMBER:

SOMETHING I LEARNED ABOUT MYSELF

My Sermon Notes

BIBLE PASSAGE

Book:

Chapter:

Verse(s):

Speaker:

Location:

WHAT I LEARNED

Who are the main characters in the passage?

What does God want me to learn?

How should I change because of this sermon?

My favorite worship song today:

Today I want to pray for:

DRAW A PICTURE OR WRITE SOMETHING YOU HEARD IN THE SERMON

My Sermon Notes

	YES!	NO!
Did you read your Bible this week?	☐	☐
Did you still remember last week's sermon?	☐	☐
Can you say a verse you have learned recently?	☐	☐

BIBLE PASSAGE: **DATE:**

CATCH THE WORD: Check the box each time you hear the word.

☐ God   ☐ Pray   ☐ Obey
☐ Love   ☐ Hope   ☐ Faith
☐ Jesus   ☐ Savior   ☐ Repent
☐ Believe   ☐ Truth   ☐ Joy

TODAY'S SERMON IS ABOUT..

APPLICATION

I should..

I should not..

DRAW A PICTURE OF SOMETHING YOU HEARD IN THE SERMON

My Sermon Notes

Date:

Speaker:

Today's Scripture?

Book:

Chapter:

Verse(s):

How do you watch the sermon?

3 BIG THINGS I LEARNED TODAY:

Who you watched the sermon with?

Words I don't know:

DRAW A PICTURE OF SOMETHING YOU HEARD IN THE SERMON

BARN LIFE!

SERMON NOTES

Date: _____   Speaker: _____

Bible Scripture: _____

3 WORDS I HEARD MORE THAN ONCE:

1.

2.

3.

WHAT ARE YOU LEARNING ABOUT GOD FROM THIS SERMON?

I can use this in my life by..

WORDS I HEARD BUT DON'T KNOW:

MY FAVORITE WORSHIP SONG TODAY:

A GOOD VERSE TO REMEMBER:

SOMETHING I LEARNED ABOUT MYSELF

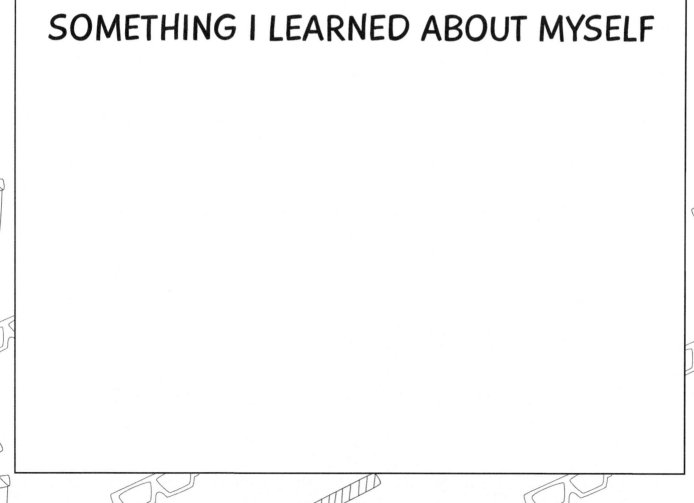

My Sermon Notes

BIBLE PASSAGE

Book:

Chapter:

Verse(s):

Speaker:

Location:

WHAT I LEARNED

Who are the main characters in the passage?

What does God want me to learn?

How should I change because of this sermon?

My favorite worship song today:

Today I want to pray for:

DRAW A PICTURE OR WRITE SOMETHING YOU HEARD IN THE SERMON

My Sermon Notes

	YES!	NO!
Did you read your Bible this week?	☐	☐
Did you still remember last week's sermon?	☐	☐
Can you say a verse you have learned recently?	☐	☐

BIBLE PASSAGE: DATE:

CATCH THE WORD: Check the box each time you hear the word.

☐ God   ☐ Pray   ☐ Obey
☐ Love   ☐ Hope   ☐ Faith
☐ Jesus   ☐ Savior   ☐ Repent
☐ Believe   ☐ Truth   ☐ Joy

TODAY'S SERMON IS ABOUT..

APPLICATION

I should..

I should not..

DRAW A PICTURE OF SOMETHING YOU HEARD IN
THE SERMON

My Sermon Notes

Date:

Speaker:

Today's Scripture?

Book:

Chapter:

Verse(s):

How do you watch the sermon?

3 BIG THINGS I LEARNED TODAY:

Who you watched the sermon with?

Words I don't know:

DRAW A PICTURE OF SOMETHING YOU HEARD IN THE SERMON

SERMON NOTES

Date: _____

Speaker: _____

Bible Scripture: _____

3 WORDS I HEARD MORE THAN ONCE:

1.

2.

3.

WHAT ARE YOU LEARNING ABOUT GOD FROM THIS SERMON?

I can use this in my life by..

WORDS I HEARD BUT DON'T KNOW:

MY FAVORITE
WORSHIP SONG TODAY:

A GOOD VERSE
TO REMEMBER:

SOMETHING I LEARNED ABOUT MYSELF

My Sermon Notes

BIBLE PASSAGE

Book:

Chapter:

Verse(s):

Speaker:

Location:

WHAT I LEARNED

Who are the main characters in the passage?

What does God want me to learn?

How should I change because of this sermon?

BEST NURSE EVER!

My favorite worship song today:

Today I want to pray for:

HERE TO HELP!

DRAW A PICTURE OR WRITE SOMETHING YOU HEARD IN THE SERMON

My Sermon Notes

	YES!	NO!
Did you read your Bible this week?	☐	☐
Did you still remember last week's sermon?	☐	☐
Can you say a verse you have learned recently?	☐	☐

BIBLE PASSAGE: DATE:

CATCH THE WORD: Check the box each time you hear the word.

☐ God   ☐ Pray   ☐ Obey
☐ Love   ☐ Hope   ☐ Faith
☐ Jesus   ☐ Savior   ☐ Repent
☐ Believe   ☐ Truth   ☐ Joy

TODAY'S SERMON IS ABOUT..

APPLICATION

I should..

I should not..

DRAW A PICTURE OF SOMETHING YOU HEARD IN THE SERMON

My Sermon Notes

Date:

Speaker:

Today's Scripture?

Book:

Chapter:

Verse(s):

How do you watch the sermon?

3 BIG THINGS I LEARNED TODAY:

Who you watched the sermon with?

Words I don't know:

DRAW A PICTURE OF SOMETHING YOU HEARD IN THE SERMON

SERMON NOTES

Date: _____   Speaker: _____

Bible Scripture: _____

3 WORDS I HEARD MORE THAN ONCE:

1. _____

2. _____

3. _____

WHAT ARE YOU LEARNING ABOUT GOD FROM THIS SERMON?

I can use this in my life by..

WORDS I HEARD BUT DON'T KNOW:

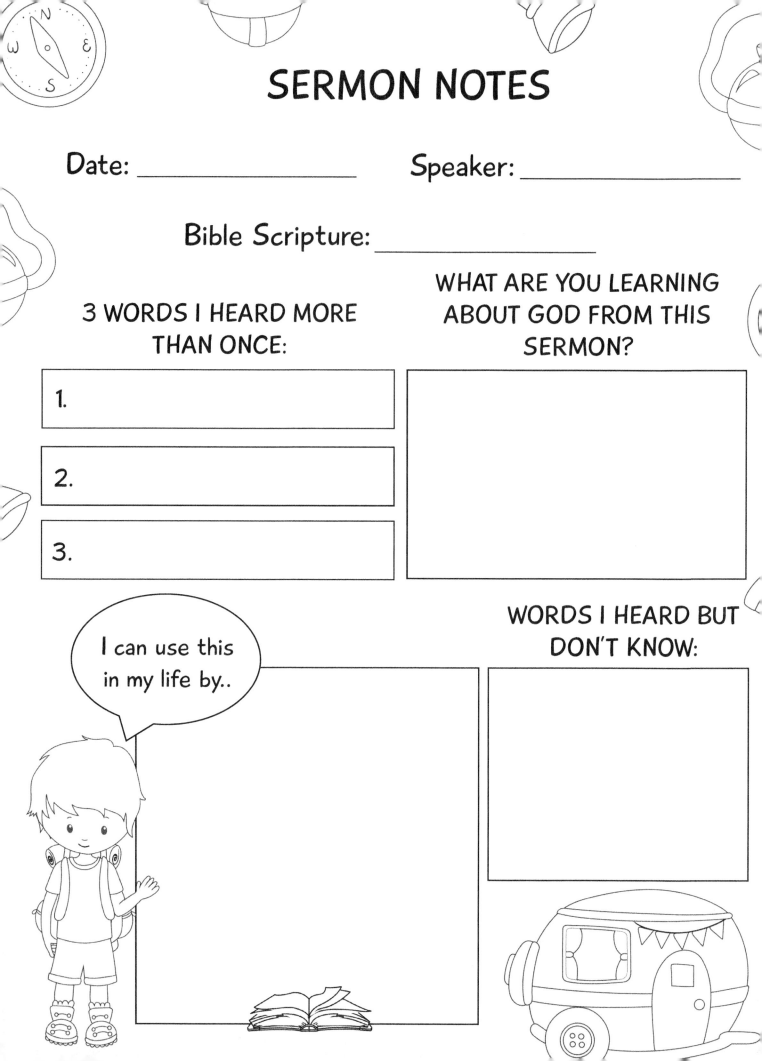

MY FAVORITE WORSHIP SONG TODAY:

A GOOD VERSE TO REMEMBER:

SOMETHING I LEARNED ABOUT MYSELF

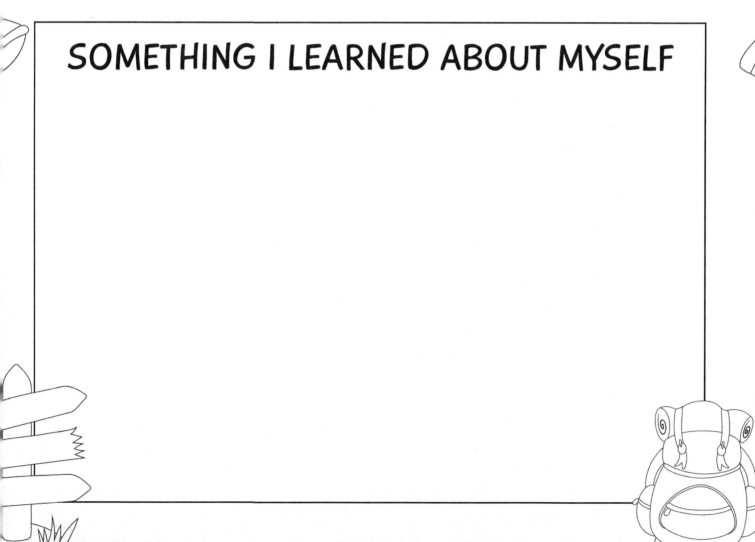

My Sermon Notes

BIBLE PASSAGE

Book:

Chapter:

Verse(s):

Speaker:

Location:

WHAT I LEARNED

Who are the main characters in the passage?

What does God want me to learn?

I ♡ LONDON

How should I change because of this sermon?

My favorite worship song today:

Today I want to pray for:

DRAW A PICTURE OR WRITE SOMETHING YOU HEARD IN THE SERMON

PLACE TO VISIT

PLACE TO VISIT

PLACE TO VISIT

LONDON

PLACE TO VISIT

My Sermon Notes

	YES!	NO!
Did you read your Bible this week?	☐	☐
Did you still remember last week's sermon?	☐	☐
Can you say a verse you have learned recently?	☐	☐

BIBLE PASSAGE: **DATE:**

CATCH THE WORD: Check the box each time you hear the word.

- ☐ God
- ☐ Love
- ☐ Jesus
- ☐ Believe

- ☐ Pray
- ☐ Hope
- ☐ Savior
- ☐ Truth

- ☐ Obey
- ☐ Faith
- ☐ Repent
- ☐ Joy

TODAY'S SERMON IS ABOUT..

APPLICATION

I should..

I should not..

DRAW A PICTURE OF SOMETHING YOU HEARD IN THE SERMON

My Sermon Notes

Date:

Speaker:

Today's Scripture?

Book:

Chapter:

Verse(s):

How do you watch
the sermon?

3 BIG THINGS I
LEARNED TODAY:

Who you watched
the sermon with?

Words I don't know:

DRAW A PICTURE OF SOMETHING YOU HEARD IN THE SERMON

SERMON NOTES

Date: _____

Speaker: _____

Bible Scripture: _____

3 WORDS I HEARD MORE THAN ONCE:

1.

2.

3.

WHAT ARE YOU LEARNING ABOUT GOD FROM THIS SERMON?

I can use this in my life by..

WORDS I HEARD BUT DON'T KNOW:

MY FAVORITE WORSHIP SONG TODAY:

A GOOD VERSE TO REMEMBER:

SOMETHING I LEARNED ABOUT MYSELF

My Sermon Notes

BIBLE PASSAGE

Book:

Chapter:

Verse(s):

Speaker:

Location:

WHAT I LEARNED

Who are the main characters in the passage?

What does God want me to learn?

How should I change because of this sermon?

My favorite worship song today:

Today I want to pray for:

DRAW A PICTURE OR WRITE SOMETHING YOU HEARD IN THE SERMON

My Sermon Notes

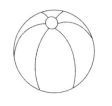

	YES!	NO!
Did you read your Bible this week?	☐	☐
Did you still remember last week's sermon?	☐	☐
Can you say a verse you have learned recently?	☐	☐

BIBLE PASSAGE: **DATE:**

CATCH THE WORD: Check the box each time you hear the word.

☐ God   ☐ Pray   ☐ Obey
☐ Love   ☐ Hope   ☐ Faith
☐ Jesus   ☐ Savior   ☐ Repent
☐ Believe   ☐ Truth   ☐ Joy

TODAY'S SERMON IS ABOUT..

APPLICATION

I should..

I should not..

DRAW A PICTURE OF SOMETHING YOU HEARD IN THE SERMON

My Sermon Notes

Date:

Speaker:

Today's Scripture?

Book:

Chapter:

Verse(s):

How do you watch the sermon?

3 BIG THINGS I LEARNED TODAY:

Who you watched the sermon with?

Words I don't know:

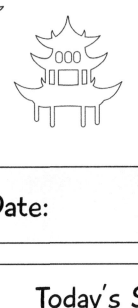

DRAW A PICTURE OF SOMETHING YOU HEARD IN THE SERMON

SERMON NOTES

Date: _____ Speaker: _____

Bible Scripture: _____

3 WORDS I HEARD MORE THAN ONCE:

1.

2.

3.

WHAT ARE YOU LEARNING ABOUT GOD FROM THIS SERMON?

I can use this in my life by..

WORDS I HEARD BUT DON'T KNOW:

MY FAVORITE WORSHIP SONG TODAY:

A GOOD VERSE TO REMEMBER:

SOMETHING I LEARNED ABOUT MYSELF

My Sermon Notes

BIBLE PASSAGE

Book:

Chapter:

Verse(s):

Speaker:

Location:

WHAT I LEARNED

Who are the main characters in the passage?

What does God want me to learn?

How should I change because of this sermon?

My favorite worship song today:

Today I want to pray for:

DRAW A PICTURE OR WRITE SOMETHING YOU HEARD IN THE SERMON

My Sermon Notes

	YES!	NO!
Did you read your Bible this week?	☐	☐
Did you still remember last week's sermon?	☐	☐
Can you say a verse you have learned recently?	☐	☐

BIBLE PASSAGE: DATE:

CATCH THE WORD: Check the box each time you hear the word.

☐ God   ☐ Pray   ☐ Obey
☐ Love   ☐ Hope   ☐ Faith
☐ Jesus   ☐ Savior   ☐ Repent
☐ Believe ☐ Truth   ☐ Joy

TODAY'S SERMON IS ABOUT..

APPLICATION

I should..

I should not..

DRAW A PICTURE OF SOMETHING YOU HEARD IN THE SERMON

Printed in Great Britain
by Amazon

40917329R00064